Table of Contents: 79 things you need to know about Estate Sales

#22-Clothing racks
#23-Display cases
#24-Signage
#25-Placing the signs
#26-Smaller items needed
#27-Advertising your sale in the paper
#28-Paid online advertising
#29-Free online advertising
#30-Pre-selling the sale
#31-Items that need pre-selling/guns
#32-Gold and silver coins
#33-Oil canvas paintings
#34-Motor vehicles/boats
#35-Sterling
#36-10k-12k-14k-18k-Gold jewelry
#37-Pricing furniture
#38-Pricing china
#39-Pricing work tools
#40-Pricing pianos
#41-Pricing string instruments
#42-Pricing wind instruments
#43-Guitars
#44-Hiding in plain sight
#45-VHSs-CDs-DVDs
#46-Kitchen appliances
#47-Other kitchen stuff
#48-Silver plate
#49-Middle Eastern rugs
#50-American Indian rugs
#51-Recent American rugs
#52-Old Chinese rugs
#53-New Chinese rugs
#54-Art Nouveau Lithos
#55-Deco lithos
#56-Modern lithos/Serigraphs
#57-Movie posters, lobbies, and song sheets
#58-Japanese woodblock prints/Ubiyo-e
#59-Old Chinese artifacts
#60-Old German/Swiss artifacts

PREFACE:

When my wife and I started an Estate Sale Service based in Malibu, CA, more than 15 years ago, we could not imagine the large need for this service. Besides the many Estate Sales we held in Malibu, we serviced sales from Brentwood to Santa Barbara. We have seen it all, from estates with 23 cars littering the property, to Hoarder Sales with gold coins worth over one million dollars. REMEMBER THESE WORDS: DON'T THROW ANYTHING AWAY! What looks like a rusty old toy could be worth hundreds to thousands. We will try to help the reader gain the insight we now have without the same amount of time involvement or elbow grease.

There are many reasons to have an Estate Sale. The most usual reasons are Death of a Family Member, Divorce or Moving. De-cluttering and Down-sizing are other valid reasons but usually on a smaller scale. Those might be better handled by a Moving Sale or Garage Sale.

The differences between an Estate Sale, Moving Sale and a Garage Sale are these: A Garage sale offers what is for sale in the garage. It is limited to the Garage. A Moving sale is what's for sale that you can't take with you. It could happen in a yard, garage, or part of a house. An Estate Sale is different because EVERYTHING in the entire house is for sale. It also includes the garage and the yard.

This book is for anyone who needs Estate Sale Services. It is also for anyone wanting to run their own sale or...... to enter this exciting and lucrative business. It will show what is expected from all those different angles.

We wish to emphasize that what follows in this book are only our own opinions, what we have found true about our Estate Sales. Your own experience may vary or be different!

#1: A death in the family

This is always a hard time for the family. A relative has passed away leaving all of their effects in their home. Sorting through all those things can be daunting. It can also be heart breaking. Hiring an Estate Sale Service can let you relax and let The Service do all the "heavy lifting." It is also the best way to divide up the Estate among those named in the will. It makes sure there is equal value for the survivors. Someone in the family may want something that is much more valuable. How do you divide up a piano for instance? An Estate Sale Service can appraise and assign a value to everything! That way the distribution of the estate is equitable.

#2: Divorce

An Estate Sale Service is the impartial way to divide assets between spouses that can't make their marriage work anymore. The Service can be trusted and the results can be split down the middle. This just includes the commonly purchased items such as art, furniture, kitchen items, and anything else that wasn't given as a gift to the other. This does not include items that belonged to either before they were married. It only includes what was acquired while married. Having an Estate Sale service do this will eliminate any haggling or worse between the principals.

#3 De-cluttering, Moving, Down-sizing

Over the years, we accumulate many things that seemed important at the time. Eventually, keeping all of this "stuff" reaches critical mass. It is like the Marx brothers film "Room Service." Groucho keeps inviting more and more people into the room until finally when the last person tries to enter, they all spill backwards out of it. When you finally realize that your residence is cluttered, it is time to divest. If you have lots of money, it is called collecting instead of hoarding. In either case, you have too much stuff.

When we move, there are certain items that don't need to go with you. Culling these out will help the bottom line with the move. If the move is into a smaller residence, down-sizing, it becomes very important to get rid of as much as you can't live without.

Depending on the scope of these reasons to divest, you may need Estate Sale Services. If you only have a few items or just some furniture, you may be better served to consign them or run your own sale. Most Estate Sale Companies require a certain amount of value before they will even want to hold your sale. They do have expenses from staff to advertising and take all the risk.

#4-Making Contact (hiring a company)

We know from experience that different internet search engines charge for placement of Estate Sale Companies ads when you are searching. When a company comes up first in the search, it doesn't mean that the company has been in business longer, but just pays the search engine company, like Google or Bing, more for a higher listing. When you look for a company, look at their private web-site. Find out how long they have been doing business. Ask for references. Put your town in the search engine such as: Estate Sales Santa Barbara, or Estate Sales Camarillo. That way you are more likely to find a local company. A local company will know the market in your area and usually do a better job getting the locals out to your sale. Try to make sure that the company has been in business for a while, usually a few years. You don't want a new company that may be learning the trade doing your sale. Younger companies may offer you less of a commission cost but You Get What You Pay For! Select what looks like the top three companies for your interviews. You want to interview at least three companies.

#5-What to expect making the call

When you call an Estate Sale Company, make sure they are available for the dates you want to hold the sale. If not, call the next company. They will want to qualify you to see if it is worth their time to even do an interview. They will want to know what you will have in the sale. If you can email them pictures, so much the better. Make sure that if family members want certain items, that those are already taken away and not offered. When our Malibu company found that family members hadn't yet picked what they wanted from an estate, we were reluctant to do an interview until that had happened. Make sure that there is enough to sell in your sale after the family picking has ended. We have seen families run off with all the cream and leave all the crap. No company except a new one will do your sale then.

#6-The interview

When you contact three Estate Sale companies, try to see them within a 48 hour period. Ask them how they will market your sale. Why are they better than their competition? How many in staff will they use. What advertising will they use. How will they find and drive the people who want your items to your sale? What kind of security will they have. Are they licensed and insured? They need to have at least a State Resale License. If your home/venue doesn't have liability insurance, your company needs to have it. If a company is bonded, that only means they use different staff all the time and it isn't really a plus. Make sure you discuss exactly what you need from the company from start to finish. Is it just a sale or a complete pack out?

#7-Extreme Cleanup/Complete Pack Out

Some sale venues were so filthy when we started the preparatory set up work that we required "Extreme Clean-up" which isn't a standard service for an Estate Sale company. We saw homes where the deceased hadn't cleaned the home in months. You can't run a sale in filth because no buyer who attends will want to touch anything. "Extreme clean-up" is a different service and expect to pay extra for it.

A standard sale is just selling items from the home. It doesn't include anything other than leaving the home "broom clean". All items unsold are left where they are. If you require a "pack-out," meaning the house must be completely empty, that is an extra service as well. A pack out is removing all items, furniture, etc. from the home even if they don't sell. It requires packing up unsold items, contacting and meeting donation services who will take everything away. A pack out is usually needed if the house will be offered for sale after the estate sale. Expect to pay extra for that service.

#8-The percentage

So many people are driven by getting something for less, they overlook that they might get less service. The standard in the industry for a good full service company is 35%. You can bargain your rate lower if you have top quality items for sale. If you have less to sell, don't be surprised if a company quotes you 40%. One sliding scale of value for salable items in the house is this: for a sale with less than $5,000. 40%. From $5,001 to $10,000. 35%. From $10,001 to $15,000. 30% and above $15,000. 25%. The important thing to remember is a quality company will want the standard amount. A newer company will offer you less percentage and, again, you will get what you pay for. Inexperience and the possibility of costly mistakes won't help you!

#9-Making the choice

Go with your gut feelings. It is important to be able to work with the people you plan to hire. There are a number of things to look for. Was the company representative well dressed, clean, polite, and educated? Did he/she show up on time for the appointment? Did they instill a feeling of trust in you? Would you want them to run your sale? Remember that you are hiring people who will be working in your home, quite often when you aren't there. Did they seem relaxed during the interview? Will they have enough staff to do the job right? Don't be pressured by any company into making your choice! If they are pressuring you before they have done anything, imagine how they will be later!

#10-Number of Sale Days

Depending on how much stuff you have to sell, that should determine how many days you have a sale. If your sale is small, less than $5,000 worth of items, a one day sale should work fine. The average sale is 2 days and has between $5,000 to $12,000 worth of salable merchandise. If you have $12,000 to $20,000 3 days is really enough to move the bulk of that estate. More than $20,000 could use four days but most companies will want 35% because of their expenses for staff. If they have lowered their percentage because you have more than $20,000 worth of items, they will baulk at a fourth day for 25%. Hold the sale on consecutive days, not split over 2 weekends. Anyone who makes a living by buying at Estate Sales won't show up 2 weeks in a row.

#11-Which Days?

A one day sale is good for either Friday or Saturday, but we lean toward Saturday. A two day sale is best served running Friday and Saturday. Our company found that Friday brought dealers and people who had seen the ads and were looking for a particular item. Saturday is the big Garage Sale day and there will be buyers cruising the streets, looking for action when they see your signage. They may not have read an ad about your sale. We had people drop in and buy when they were on their way to the dentist! A three day sale, our company found best served running Thursday, Friday, and Saturday. A four day sale found Thursday, Friday, Saturday and Sunday working well. You may wonder why Sunday wasn't listed in the first three examples. People usually have plans for Sunday. They go to church, sports events, or just want to vegetate at home. Sunday was always slower in sales for us.

#12-Staffing the Sale

You will need an efficient cashier, garage guy, security doorman, and at least 2 roaming people for the standard sale. If you have lots of jewelry, gold, silver, or other valuable items, you will also need a "jewelry cage" seller. The roamers are like your neighborhood watch. They make sure everything is on the up and up. If the home has an upstairs and downstairs, add one more roamer. It is important to have enough staff especially on the first day of a sale. The first two hours can be crazy!

#13 Duties of a Cashier

The cashier should be good with numbers. He/she should have at least 2 calculators and a running tally accounting book of everything that is paid for. Accounting books are available at most stationary stores like Staples or Office Depot. The running tally should list all major items such as pieces of furniture or specific art objects. If someone buys 5 books, the cashier only needs to list "5 books", not the name of each book. Kitchen items can be entered as "miscellaneous kitchen." The cashier needs to be even tempered and un-frazzled. As stated before, the first hours of a sale can be quite a test. Consider having a second cashier for the first hour. That way you can handle sales faster and buyers, waiting to exit, will be less frustrated. Having a staging table near the cashier table is questionable. People will stack things there and run off. The cashier can't baby sit the buyers purchases.

#14- The Running Tally

You need an accounting book for the cashier for a running tally. This is the bible of how a company reports receipts to the client. The cashier needs to have neat writing and good penmanship. Telling the difference between a 4 and a 9, or a 1 and a 7 are important. At the end of the day, the running tally needs to balance with the cash/check/credit card total. The accounting book should make at least 2 copies. You will be handing one copy to the client when you settle with them. If you go with 2 cashiers at the beginning of your sale, you need 2 accounting books. The book should have the day and date written in for each day of the sale. Totals should be entered for each day.

#15-Duties of a Garage Guy

Malibu Surplus found that most tools, sports equipment, CDs, DVDs, picture frames, and basically more junky items belong in the garage. Your garage guy should know how all the tools work. Your garage guy should know for what price all things in the garage are selling. At the beginning of the sale, the garage should not be opened or the garage guy will be overwhelmed. As you might not have had enough time to price everything in the whole garage, your guy should have pricing labels to place on unpriced items so the cashier will know what to charge. After the first 2 hours of the sale, when things have calmed down, the garage guy can open the garage and operate separatly from the rest of the house. When this happens, he will be his own cashier for all he sells. He also needs to have a running tally at that point. He should greet all new buyers by saying: "everything in the house is for sale". That way those buyers won't think the garage is the whole sale.

#16-Duties of Roamers

Having the right number of roamers for a sale is crucial. Your roamers should have the ability to price any item. No matter how many items you price with tags and stickers, you will miss a few. Tags and stickers also fall off or are pulled off by buyers trying to cheat the sale. A very small number of buyers also figure that they should have something from the sale for free. Beware of people in large bulky coats, especially in warm weather, and ladies with huge handbags. We have asked people to check those at the door upon entry to the sale. Roamers are the watch dogs to keep people from pocketing small items. They also straighten up items such as clothes that have fallen off the rack or shoes that have been thrown in all directions. It is their responsibility to keep the sale looking neat and fresh.

#17-Duties of the Security / Doorman

The security/doorman should be of imposing size, enough to be obeyed or respected, like a bouncer at a club. If you have lots of interesting items and have done a good job advertising the sale, there should be a line of people waiting to get in on the first day. Make sure to leave a sign-up sheet outside the night before the sale. Our company had 80 people waiting for one sale in Malibu. The doorman will make sure that only a few people get in at first. Depending on the size of the home, we found that 5-15 was a good number to start with. The doorman will go out and explain to the crowd the precise number he will let in. When those people leave, he will regulate how many more to let in. He can also inform them that baggy coats and large purses will either not be allowed inside or must be checked with him. We found numbered clothes pins worked well. There are two pins for each checked item and the buyer keeps one. When we had lots of valuable things at one sale, we hired a retired policeman who was actually armed. This usually isn't necessary.

#18-Duties of a Jewelry Cage Seller

If your sale has gold, silver, or other precious items, a jewelry cage is essential. It can be in a separate room that has nothing else in it. It can also be in the home's large room with tables on three sides and a wall on the fourth. The most precious items should be under glass in a case. If the "cage" is in a separate room, a roamer can guard the door and only let two people in at one time. Your cage seller should not deal with more than one person at a time. That way they can keep track of anything a buyer wants to handle. There will be pressure from other buyers to view your wares. If the cage is not in a private room but where the rest of the sale is happening, then the security person can help out the jewelry seller. Again, the first hours of a sale can be tough.

#19-Wages for your staff

The cashier is the most important position and the most stressful job at an Estate Sale. Plan to pay your cashier at least $20 more than anyone else. Our company paid our staff $15 per hour for pre-sale set up and after sale duties. Our sales ran typically 6 hours and we paid a flat $100 to all workers except the cashier who was paid $120. We expected everyone to arrive the first day at least ½ hour before the sale started.

#20-Equipment needed for a sale

There are certain items needed for a successful sale. They include folding tables, clothing racks, display boxes, pricing tags and stickers, several accounting books (that make at least 2 copies), several calculators, pens, street signs, caution tape, blue tape, bags and boxes.

#21-Folding Tables

Although you can stage an Estate Sale without folding tables, it isn't as favorable for displaying and selling you wares. Folding tables with black cloth covers in the home, makes items stand out. The idea is to move more expensive items on to a table that shows them off. It also keeps the sale from looking too cluttered. Folding tables are a must in the garage. Those don't need covers. Set up your tables so that movement can flow around them. Good inexpensive tables are for sale at Costco and Sam's Club, or check for used ones on Craigslist.com.

#22 Clothing Racks

Most sales have lots of clothes. Industrial strength clothing racks are a must for any Estate Sale Company. They can be found on sites such as Craigslist.com. The idea is to get the clothes out of the closet and out into the open. If there are tons of clothes and only a clothing rack or two, display the quality, more expensive clothing on the racks,, and leave the rest available to be seen in the closet. Leather coats, skirts and pants go on the rack. Quality wool suits, wool sweaters, and wool shirts go on the rack. Clothing on the rack needs to be tag priced. Prices should be about 20% of what it would cost new. The clothes in the closet can be bulk priced. Here's an example of a bulk pricing sign: YOUR CHOICE, $4. EACH.

#23-Display Cases

We have already noted the value of Jewelry cases but having other small quality items under glass is a valuable thing for security. If it is small and worth more than $10 it is a candidate for the display case. That also makes the small item look more desirable. Buying folding tables, clothing racks, and display cases can add to your cost if you want to do your own sale. If you are trying to decide if you want to do the sale yourself, a good Estate Sale Company already has all of the aforementioned equipment.

#24-Signage

This is one piece of equipment that is a must for anyone doing a sale. On the days the sale is happening, placing signs out on the surrounding streets to drive buyers to the sale will result in more than 50% of your business. Signs need to say: "Estate Sale" and have an arrow pointing in the direction you want the traffic to turn. You can have homemade signs but professional ones look better. Professional signs are available at home improvement stores such as Home Depot or Lowes. Signs are also available online. Professional signs will cost an average of $10 each. Make sure to have more than enough signs as they tend to disappear in some neighborhoods. One sale we did in a restricted neighborhood, had signs removed by security patrols each day. We complained to the Homeowners Association and were told the signs would be returned, but they never were.

#25-Placing the Signs

If you live within a mile or so of a major road or freeway, it is important to have signage at the exits to let drivers know about your sale. Many times a person is on the way to the dentist/store/market/school, and the sign will cause them to drop into your sale. Make sure that at important turns, when you need to direct the traffic left or right, that you have 2 signs in different spots pointing the way. Sometimes disgruntled neighbors will knock down a sign on their side, but rarely knock down two. You will know if someone has messed with your signs. A few hours into the sale, no new buyers will have appeared. At that point, have a roamer go and check. All the advertising you might use will only have people come to the beginning of your sale. After that, your signs are THE major source of most new buyers!

#26-Smaller items needed

Besides the large stuff, there are lots of little items needed. Pricing tags for clothes, pricing stickers for smaller sale items, accounting books (available at stationary stores) caution tape to seal off any unwanted access areas, blue tape to mark off stairs or sudden drop off areas, and bags and boxes for your buyers.

#27-Advertising your Sale in The Paper

If you happen to live in a large city, there are usually several different ways to advertise. The major paper is the most obvious source of exposure. I happen to know that a major paper will charge more for an "Estate Sale" ad than a "Garage Sale" advertisement. The LA Times, for instance, charges twice as much for an estate sale ad. Our company found that the "Garage Sale Ad" worked just as well at getting the word out and at a fraction of the cost. You can even title the garage sale ad: Estate Sale, Everything Must Go. There may also be other "throw-away" weekly papers that can be used to get the word out.

#28-Paid Online Advertising

The "Holy Grails" of online advertising are the two web-sites: Estatesales.net and Estatesales.org. These sites can be used weeks in advance to let professional buyers and bargain hunters know when your sale will happen. If you don't have an account with either, you may buy a onetime presence on their site for around $50. $50.spent on either company will get you around 75 pictures that can be loaded up to show what you have to sell. The site will show the dates, and you can add a description to each picture of each item available. Estatesales.net and Org will also hold back the address until the day before the sale so you won't have early birds showing up, trying to get a jump on everyone else. If your budget is limited, use Estatesales.org. They team up with Craigslist and place your ad there as well for no additional money. It is done automatically.

#29-Free Online Advertising

Just about everyone knows that Craigslist doesn't cost a dime to advertise. Because they are location specific, you may need to put several ads up with them. Again, all it costs is your time. Another lesser known site is GSALR.COM. They deal primarily with garage sales but you can still advertise for free. Many neighborhoods have a web-site with "patch" at the end of it, Malibupatch for instance. Here is another free source.

#30-Pre-selling the Sale

After you have put your online ads up with pictures of the sale, don't be surprised if you get contacted by a buyer who is willing to pay full price for a special item. There are two schools of thought about pre-selling. Firstly, if you sell something that has been advertised before the Estate Sale, there may be a buyer who drives a long way to the Estate Sale to find his item pre-sold. They won't be happy with you. If the pre-sale is at least a week before the sale, just delete the picture from your ad and there is no problem. The second school of thought is: never let a buyer get away! Sell when you can. Take the money while it is there! If a person has cash and wants an item, make the sale!

#31-Items that need pre-selling-Guns

Guns can't be sold legally at any sale. There are legal gun brokers such as Lock-Stock-& Barrel who will either put your guns in a month long online auction, or buy them out right from you. These dealers are registered with the Government. You aren't. Our company derived over $10,000 from one auction that featured only 4 guns: a 1860s Navy Colt pistol, a 1911 Army Officer's 45 pistol, a 357 Magnum unfired, and a Walther PPK of James Bond fame, new in the box.

#32-Gold & Silver Coins

Some estates can have amazing collections of gold and silver coins. Depending on the size of the collection, you might be better served to pre-sell the collection or put it up to auction. If there are only a few coins, leaving them in the sale can drive more customers to you, even if it might be a headache for the Jewelry Cashier. With gold and silver coins, there is value depending on the year minted and the condition of the coin. If the coin is in poor condition, it is worth at least the spot price of the metal. The value is then measured by how many grams the coin weights. Most gold coins are 20K or better in purity. To get a fair price, figure the spot price divided by 31.103 grams per troy ounce. For example, if the spot price is $1,100. a troy ounce, divide the spot price by 31.103 and you have the price per gram. If your coin weights 20 grams, multiply the price per gram by 20.

US silver coins are .900 pure in contrast to sterling at .925. US coins minted in San Francisco or Carson City are more often rare. Use the same process if the coin is worn to find the melt value. Buying a book that has values for rarer dates is a good idea if you have many silver coins.

#-33 Oil Canvas Paintings

Let's say your sale has oil canvas art work. Oils by known artists can be worth lots of money. Unfortunately, what something is worth and what someone will pay at a sale are two different things. We saw paintings worth over $1000 sell for only a few hundred at our sales. Your oil may be a candidate for pre-sale. The first thing to establish about your oil is if it something more special than that of a common oil sold at an airport or convention hall "en masse". Look in the lower corners of an oil to find the artist's signature. When you find that, see if the artist is listed in one of the books available in many libraries that list artists of note or use the name in a google search. If your artist is listed and well thought of, it is advisable to contact an auction house that deals in oils. Houses such a Sothebys, Christies, Butterfields, and Bonhams are just a few names. By sending a picture online to an auction house, you will find if the work is worthy of being pre-sold out of the sale.

If your oil isn't wanted by an auction house, it can still be sold in your sale. How good is it? Are the brush strokes broad or very fine? Is it whimsical? Smaller oils can fetch $20-50 while larger ones $50-100. If you have a Thomas Kinkade, don't get too excited! His "oils" were mass produced by machines and touched up in spots by assistants. Even the biggest and best of his works only gets $100 at a sale.

#34-Motor Vehicles and Boats

Here is an excellent example of something to pre-sell. Many estates have Cars, Trucks, RVs, Tractors, and Boats on Trailers. The company commission rate for these items is less, usually 10 to 15%. If you have the pink-slip, you don't need to register the vehicle/boat in the Estate Sale

Companies name. All that is needed is a death certificate and proof of the Executor's name to sign the pink slip .We figured we would tell you about the legal way to transfer title. We know of other Estate Sale Companies who have just signed the decease's name on the pink slip. The Department of Motor Vehicles wasn't the wiser.

By placing an ad in the local paper, Craigslist, or Auto trader style magazine, it is easy to sell your vehicle/boat. We have sold cars with damage without any trouble at all. One sale we did in Malibu had 23 vehicles strewn out on 2 acres. Our clients needed them all to go away as the house was to be sold after the sale. We sold the ones that ran but some were really junk. The local towing company wanted $9,000 to tow the junk away. However, when we offered the towing company the pink slips to the junkers, they towed them all off at no charge.

#35-Sterling

Many estates have a set of flatware. Many flatware sets are just silver-plate and only worth what someone will pay. Sterling sets are worth the spot price of silver by gram weight. If you are a company, remember that the sterling flatware set may have sentimental value to your client. Don't tell them that you intend to sell it for melt value, even though that is only what it is worth. Consider their feelings and say you will try to get top dollar. If you have a lot of sterling, it could be pre-sold. All sterling is marked with "Sterling" embedded on the underside of the flatware, or 925. English sterling is marked with a lion. You will need a gram scale and they can be found on Ebay for around $15. Each piece will need to be weighed. When the spot price of silver is around $16 per ounce, the gram price of sterling is 40-45 cents. By showing and labeling the sterling in your online ad, you can indicate that it is available for pre-sale. If you don't pre-sell it and leave it in the ad, it will bring precious metal buyers to your sale.

#36-10K-12K-14K-18-K-Dental Gold & Jewelry

Every sale our company did had some form of gold jewelry. There are the usual 10K gold pins of various organizations, 12-14-18K rings, bracelets, chains and earpieces. Dental Gold is usually 18K. There are many jewelry pieces that look good but are just plate. Unless you have a chemical testing kit, you will need to find a Karat marking on the item. You will need a loop (Jewelers small magnifying glass) so you don't go blind squinting. Again, you will need a gram scale to figure out the melt value. Melt value is just about all these pieces are really worth. When the spot price of gold is around $1,200. These are approximate values per gram: 10K-$14. 12K-$18. 14K-$22. 18K-$26. Price your sale jewelry accordingly.

#37-Pricing Furniture

You may have lots of furniture in your sale. The non-antique pieces may be from excellent makers. The thing to remember is: IT IS USED, NOT NEW,... PRICE IT LOW. Dining room sets may be made from excellent wood but these tend to be the hardest to move. A set that might have cost $2,000 new will have a hard time going out the door for $500. The people who are buying furniture these days are usually young professionals between the ages of 25-45. They drive the market. Their tastes are different than the boomers or even gen-xers. Keep chanting the mantra: "They are paying you to clear out the house."   Sometimes we have sold cloth sofas for as little as $30. Leather sofas do go for more but not more than a few hundred. Antique chairs fare better but you are very lucky to get even $50 a chair. Nice dressers go for $200. Bedroom sets need to be priced low to have a chance of selling. Otherwise, you may have a lot of donations on your hands after the sale.

#38-Pricing China

Here is another white elephant. Sets of fine china have languished at many an estate sale. Even respected names don't move unless priced at give-away prices. We have sold large sets of Noritake for only $80. We have had sets of French Limoges china. There are around 80 makers from this region so find out which you have. Even great Limoges has been left over in sales, even with a bargain price on it. The exception to "white elephant china" has been Fiesta ware, Bauer ware, Catalina Island, California Rainbow, and other companies that made their colorful ware in the 20s and 30s. Those are highly collectable. If you are lucky enough to have any early collectables, you can use Ebay to price them. Look on the left hand side of the selling page to find the Items Sold section. That way you will have a real idea of what something is worth. Ebay sellers price many of these items too high. Seeing what an item really sold for instead of how it was listed, gives you a starting point.

#39-Pricing Work Tools

Tools are garage items but can bring in a good amount. Power tools get the most money. Everyone has hand tools so they have to be priced cheaply. Common hammers and hand saws go for $1. Screwdrivers 50 cents. Gardening saws get more depending on size, up to $10. Pruning shears get $5 to 10. Shovels and rakes are $3-5. Sledge hammers: Sm-$5 Lg-$10. Picks-$8 Crowbars-$4......you get the picture. Power tools such as Skill Saws, Ryobi and Makita can bring in big bucks. We sold a large Skill saw for $80. Drills are common and only get $10. Electric trimmers- $20. Gas powered trimmers $40. Table saws can bring in over $100 depending on size. We had a $2000, when new, table saw that finally sold for $500. If you have a good Garage Guy, then he will know all of this anyway and price the items to move. Over pricing will just leave you with more stuff to deal with at the end of the sale.

#40-Pricing Pianos

Having a piano in your sale is a dubious honor. Unless it is a famous name brand like Steinway, you will be trying to unload it cheap as it costs a small fortune to move. To find out what you really have, the first thing to do is to test the action of every key. Make sure they all work and the key comes back into place with all the others. Does the piano sound in tune? Tuning a piano is now $100 or more. You don't want to do that. You are in the business of selling, not repairing! Put your foot on each pedal and play a key to see that the pedals work. Many older pianos need either new strings or work on the key action. Again, you don't want to do that. Leave that to the person who is taking the piano away. Sometimes a family won't care about any of the above and just want the piano for the kids to learn on OR to have the piano as a piece of furniture. In most cases, just finding someone to move it out of the house is wonderful. If you can collect $100 or more, great.

If you are lucky enough to have a Brand Name Piano in good condition, then you can start asking over a thousand or more. In the many years that our company was in business, 9 out of 10 pianos were junkers!

#41-Pricing String Instruments

There are many old violins, violas, and cellos in the attic. Most are turn of the century (1900) German made. These are worth a few hundred if they don't have cracks in them. Not having cracks goes for all string instruments. A sound post or bass bar crack will cut the value in half, even if the crack has been repaired. Most instruments will have a label that you can read by looking in the top right f-hole. Many will say Stradivarus. Don't get your hopes up! Just about all the 1,100 instruments that Antonio Stradvari made are accounted for. Don't get excited if the label says Guarnerius either. There are many copies made to look like these two Italian makers. Get excited if the label is French or any other Italian maker. If you know anyone who plays a string instrument, that is the first person to show it to. Going into a violin shop will cost $100 or more for only a verbal appraisal. Forget that most violin shops have the ethics of a used car salesman. If you have something really good, they will try to buy it from you for peanuts. Sending online pictures to an auction house like Tarisio in New York is a cheap option to find if you have something good. In any case, your string instrument, if it is a good one, could be worth thousands.

#42-Wind Instruments

Look at the condition of the flute, sax, horn, oboe, clarinet, etc. Does it look clean or is it corroded and dirty. You want clean. Is it a brand name that you recognize? There are older saxs that can be worth a few grand. If your flute is solid gold or silver, bingo!!! Wind instruments that have pads, may need those replaced. You don't want to do that. Let your buyer see the value of the axe "as-is". The idea for all instruments is to move them out, not repair them.

#43-Guitars

There can be sizable money in either acoustic or electric guitars. If your guitar is acoustic, the top names are Martin, Gibson and Taylor. Other names that are good are Fender, Yamaha, and Washburn. For electric guitars, early 1950s 1960s Fenders are worth thousands. Your kids will probably know more than you do about this. To find the value, look online at an auction site. Just like the string instruments, having cracks in your guitar isn't good!

#44-Hiding in Plain Sight

Sometimes what looks like junk is anything but. In the back yard, in a shed, in the garage, or left outside to rot lurks other precious metal: Copper and Brass. Old discolored piping could be copper. Any bundles of electric wiring also have copper. To check the pipe, does it look brown? Take a file and scratch the end. If it is copper, you will know. In fact after seeing old copper piping in its discarded state, you will become an expert. Recycling centers will pay upwards of $2 a pound for the stuff. The wiring will only bring about half that because it isn't pure with the wrapping. In one estate we found about 20 old copper pipes that brought in over $400 for the sale.

Brass is also good but it needs to be unattached to any other metal. Old sprinkler heads, gas fittings, ugly candlesticks that won't sell, door handles, pulls, wall brackets and nails can all have brass in them. To check if it is brass, hold a magnet to the suspect metal. If it isn't magnetic and looks like brass, it is. Recycling centers will pay over a $1 per pound. The same sale that had the copper pipes, also had a ton of brass that brought in over $200. That sale had over $600 hiding in plain sight!

#45-VHS-CDs-DVDs

With VHS, the older cassette video tape system, you will need to have a player to sell the tapes. Our company has had all the great Disney titles in VHS but without a player, NO ONE wanted them. Our last sale with a collection of 90 Disney VHS titles sold with player for only $50. You get the picture.

CDs are a great way to augment the take of a sale. They must be in un-scratched condition to sell. Make sure you open the plastic case and that there is a disc inside. The average price for a single CD is $1.

DVDs will add even more to your sale. Depending on the title, you can get $3 for one. Most average titles are still worth $2. Again, check to make sure a disc is in the package. DVDs have a way of sneaking out of the packaging and becoming lost! The roamers need to keep an eye on CDs and DVDs as you may start your sale with both of those in the jackets, but thieves will slip the disks out and leave the jackets.

#46-Kitchen Appliances

Every kitchen has small appliances. Coffee makers, bean grinders, toaster ovens, waffle irons, and mixers to name a few. The prince of these is a Jura automatic coffee maker. That is the type where you only push one button to get your coffee. Jura coffee makers cost near $2000 when new. Espresso machines are also good sellers, but for much less money. Some mixers can help the sale. Kitchen aid is a great name. Their large mixers sell for $100 depending on condition. Toaster ovens, coffee grinders and waffle irons will only get you 10-20 dollars. The appliance must be clean and work. Make sure to test it before offering it in the sale.

#47-Other Kitchen Stuff

The pots, pans, utensils, knives, and assorted flat ware can be money makers. Any French copper pot or pan could be worth $50-100. Le Crueset pots and pans are also highly valued. Their large pots have brought in $80. Smaller stuff brings $20-40. German Hinkle knives are excellent. A set could realize over $100. Other name brand quality knives can be worth $10 each. The rule of thumb is, if it looks like a quality piece, it needs to be priced higher than the rest. Stainless flatware, if it is a complete set for 8 and has an interesting pattern can be priced for $20. Other serving pieces are strictly $1 per item fare. This includes pasta forks, pizza cutters, spatulas, large wooden spoons, and other items in plastic. The idea here is to squeeze as much money out of your kitchen items as possible. The Estate Sale Creed is: "It all adds up!"

#48-Silver Plate

Many homes have flatware and serving pieces that aren't Sterling. Silver Plate may not be as valuable but can also realize good money. The larger and more unique the piece is, the more you can charge for it. Flatware sets can sell for $60-100. "Tea Sets" which have Tea pot, Coffee pot, Sugar and Cream servers with a large matching platter can go for $50-100 depending on how unique they are. If they are before the turn of the century (1900) that is even better. Large serving spoons and forks, cake servers and the like get $3 to $5. Large serving pots and plates command $10. Large handled platters can go out the door for $20. The heavier the weight usually means better quality. Silver plate on copper is the most valuable.

#49-Middle Eastern Rugs

I know rug stores sell their foreign rugs for incredible prices, thousands of dollars. Rugs from the mid-east can be valuable. There are a lot of copies of these expensive rugs being made by machines in China. If you have a real hand tied rug from Turkey or Iran, to name just 2 countries, you might be able to get a fraction of its value at your sale. For example, the store would charge $2000 but the sale would only get $400. Remember that the rugs you are selling are USED. They may need cleaning or repair. You are not in that business. You are selling! If you aren't sure about the value, ask someone who has any knowledge to help you. Maybe even pay for a verbal appraisal if you have more than 10 rugs you suspect are valuable. One sale that our company had on Pt. Dume in Malibu featured about 20 rugs that were Lillihan and Hamidan. We had priced them at $300-400 to move them. Middle Eastern dealers were waiting in line by 6am for a 9am start. 2 dealers came to blows pulling on the same carpet. (This is another reason you might need a large doorman/security person)

#50-American Indian Rugs

The older and earlier an Indian rug was made in the USA, the better. Early Indian rugs have softer colors from plant dyes. The weave is also tighter. Again, sadly, the sale can only expect to realize about half the real value. Something a store might charge $1000 for, you will be lucky to get $400-500 for. The larger an Indian rug, the more you can charge. The rug needs to be without holes, stains, and not frayed in the corners. In other words, in good shape. American Indian rugs, if your sale has more than 3, might be another candidate for pre-sale. However, the more you leave in the sale and advertise, the more diverse and plentiful your buyers will be.

#51-Recent American Rugs

Because of the period in time, 1920-1940, and even though these rugs are mostly machine made, they can be good money makers. It is the Kitch factor at work. You won't get more than $100 or less but so what! Once more, make sure that the rug is in good condition. Holes, stains, frayed corners will make even a good one of these a "throw away". In pricing remember that you can always lower your price, but you can't raise it.

#52-Old Chinese Rugs

The ones made from pure silk are the most valuable. Most likely your rugs will be made of wool. Old large 7x9' "blue and white" Peking rugs from 1850-1900 can realize $500 or more depending on condition. If your large old Chinese rug has walking ware in the high traffic areas, it is still worth around $200. Smaller 3x5' blue and whites are worth $50.

#53-New Chinese Rugs

You have seen them at Costco or other container stores. They are large and they are beautiful. A new 4x6 will sell in the store for $400-500. Your price should be $75. A new large 7x9' will sell in the store for $1200-1600. You should price it at only $200. Many times when our company priced these rugs higher, we had them left over from the sale to donate. As the movie says: "Show me the money!" You are there to move the merchandise out of the house. You are not there to run a museum.

#54-Art Nouveau Lithos

Lithography can add a big boost to the total of a sale. Depending on who pulled the stone litho and where it was made, it could be worth thousands. Pre-turn of the century (before 1900) and up to the 1920s is where the big money comes in. Famous European artists Lautrec, Steinlen, Berton, Mucha, Cheret, Grasset, Klimt, Beardsley and Prevmont are just a few names of La Belle Epoch, the Art Nouveau movement. Their original lithos are getting harder to find. Even the older re-pro copies (from 60s 70s) of these artists can sell for hundreds. To make sure your litho is an original there are several things to look for. Smaller editions of these artists and others were published in the art book "Maitre de L'Affiche". Each of the 256 pages with a litho has an embossment of the paper in the lower right hand corner. These are all worth over $1000 if by any of the artists listed above. The other artists in that book are still worth hundreds.

Another art publication of that period was La Stampe Moderne. Again, these are small versions of larger works sent out to art collectors of that period. The same values apply.

If you are lucky enough to have a full size Art Nouveaux litho, it could really make the whole sale and definitely be a candidate for and Art Auction House. Full size Lautrecs go for $40,000-80,000. Full size Muchas go for $10,000-20,000. An example of full size would be 36"x24" or larger. If the artist has also signed the litho by hand, as well as in the stone plate, the work is more valuable.

#55-Deco Lithos

Deco was the rage during 1910-1939 and beyond. Buildings were made in that style. The Chrysler Building in New York City is a prime example as is the Wiltern Theatre in Los Angeles. There are prints and lithos from this period by such artists as Icart, Catteau, Erte', Cassandre, Sachs, Dupas, and Lempicka. Some of these artists did amazing travel posters which might fall through the cracks if you didn't know. Depending on size and condition, large works of 32" x 48" can be worth up to $3000. To get a price as great as that, your litho must have no fold marks and no foxing or discoloration. Smaller works by these artists, 24" x 18", are worth $300-400 if in excellent condition. Again, a real signature besides one in the print will add to the value.

#56-Modern Lithos/Serigraphs

There are also fantastic modern artists that produced stone and off set lithos and serigraphs. Dali, Hockney, Lichtenstein, Warhol, Max, Rauschenberg, Rusha and Nagle are a few names. What is important here is how many pulls or prints were done for the edition. Look in the lower right corner. You will see 2 sets of numbers such as: 35 / 300 or 123 / 350 . The first number is the actual number of your print. The second number is the total number of prints in the edition printed before the stone, plate (in offset lithos) or screen (in serigraphs) was destroyed. You might not see any numbers, but instead letters such as AP or AE. This means you have an Artists Proof or Artists Edition. An artist may print his work first to see how the main run will turn out. There are typically only 10-20 of these that will exist. The smaller the edition size, the second number, the more valuable the print. A print by Dali that says: 12 / 50 is worth more than one that says 12 / 500.

#57-Movie Posters, Lobbies and Song Sheets

Howard Hawks, the producer, posters are selling for thousands. Any movie poster that is lithography and not a photo print, and is the large size: 6 ft. x 3 ft. is valuable. The new-bees in Hollywood who have the money now, want those posters to class up their joint. These may be better sold at auction!

Theater lobbies are good merchandise. The usual size is around 12"x8" but they need to be old or kitch like Godzilla, to get much. If you have a picture of a major star, Brando, Fonda, Astaire, etc…on your lobbie, you have something around $20-50. If you have a "B" movie lobby, maybe it will go for $5-10.

Songs sheets from the movies are very salable. We had three song sheets from several Bogart films including "As Time Goes By" which realized $100. The standard price for most of these is $5 each.

#58-Japanese Wood Block Prints/Ubiyo-e

There are almost too many artists of this medium to list. My personal favorites include 2 early masters: Hiroshige and Hokusai. If you are lucky to have one of these masters, they are worth over $1000 depending on condition. (no stains, foxing or discoloration) A more modern master is Hasui. He died in the 1950s. His early works are pricey because the wood blocks they were pulled from were destroyed in the huge 1920s earthquake and fire in Tokyo. Later originals are worth $400-800. There are re-strikes of the later plates after he died, but they are identified by characters in the side margins. These are still worth about $150.

#59-Old Chinese Artifacts

The Chinese have been around longer than almost anyone. Early blue and white ceramic (Ming dynasty and before) work can be worth tens of thousands of dollars. This is where a trusted expert can help. An untrusted expert may pay you a grand and sell your treasure for $40,000. Later works can still be valuable. Blue and white from 1700 to 1850 can go for $1000 a large plate without chips or cracks. Rose Canton China has been made since the 1850s and is still made today. Early work is worth much more. A more modern large 15" bowl is still worth around $200. Colorful Canton Peasant China has been sold at Sothebys. Expect to get only $20 per bowl at a sale. If you get a large collection into a good auction house, that same bowl could be worth $50.

Chinese "roll" paintings are a hard sell so move them cheap. Less than $100. Chinese screens are a great item. Hand carved ones with lacquer colors have sold for over $1000. If they have jade in them, price them higher.

#60-Old German/Swiss Artifacts

Old Prussian Porcelain used to be worth 10 times more in the 60s-70s. The people who now collect it are few and dying. A lovely plate or bowl that used to get $100 now only gets $10. It is beautiful and well-made but the market is slim.

There are many grades of Cuckoo clocks. Even the best one is only worth $100 if working. Hand carved bottle stoppers are worth between $5-10 depending on age. German Beer Steins must be from 1960 or earlier to have any real value. The newer stuff is only worth around 3 dollars a stein. German wine glasses still are popular and can be worth 5 dollars a stem. If you have WW-2 German items, there is a market but I, for one, don't like to sell weapons of that war or any of the other Nazi crap! Old Swiss mountain horns, think Ricola, are a good item to feature. Old Swiss wood carvings are great to have in the sale. All of this is valued on age and condition. As stated earlier, German steel knives are the best!

#61-Kitch

There are so many items that fall under this category. We almost threw out some very old and broken toys made of metal. They were from 1900, German made, and brought in 100s in their broken state. Everyone has seen the 1920s print: Dogs playing poker. Believe it or not, that original print is worth $60-80. Old Godzilla items are HOT! Anything from the 50s that says "Atomic" is hot. Early 40s 50s and 60s lunch boxes from the USA are hot also. We sold the first Beatles lunch box for $100. Ties and socks from that period bring the money in. Any original picture of Betty Page is worth lots. The same with Marilyn Monroe. Semi-nude 8x10" photos from the 50s, if you care to deal them, are around $10 each. (maybe with ebay under an assumed name?) Old model cars, planes, ships, and trains from that period have definite value. Give the National Geographics away to a library who wants them and get a valuable tax deduction for the donation. Any encyclopedias are old and unsellable. They are dumpster material. The advice here is: If it came from the 40s through the 70s, it could be valuable.

#62-Old Post Cards

Post Card collections showed up in our companies sales from time to time. Cards from pre-1900 can be very valuable. Cards that are stone litho printed are good but only worth around $1-3 dollars each. The more valuable cards are the old black and white ones with pictures of how things were back then. Cards that show old trains, planes, and automobiles can be worth $5 or more. Ships are good but for some reason, not as valuable. The same with Indian cards from the 20-30s. French post cards from 1900 can be worth $10 each. Art Nouveau cards can be worth $100. Display the cards in plastic so when handled, they won't be damaged. The cards can't have any damage or bent corners. Smudges subtract value from a card. With luck, you will have a card collector come to the sale and offer to buy the whole lot!

#63-Old Sheet Music

Stone litho song sheets from La Belle Epoch were made by some of the great Art Nouveau artists. I own 3 done by Steinlen that I bought at a Sothebys auction in the 1970s for $200.

Stone litho song sheets from old Broadway Shows also have good value and sell for $5 each. Again, make sure to case them in plastic to save them from exploring hands at the sale.

#64-Patio/Pool Stuff

Most sales will have Patio and Pool items. There will be chairs, tables, chasses, bar-b-ques, umbrellas, planters, floating chairs and rafts, skimmers, pool vacs and the like. They are all sellable. A good name like Brown and Jordan helps sell chairs and chasses. Those can sell for $25 a chair and $100 per chasse. Wrought iron chairs and tables sell well. A small table and 2 chairs can bring in $50. A large set can realize $200. We had a large tile table that weighed over 1000 pounds. It sold for $500. I can still hear the Jamaican Movers, 5 huge guys who moved that table, complaining: "Yo killin me mon!" Remember this, pool stuff is expensive when you buy it new. It can be sold for half the new price when you sell it used. Bar-b-ques are worth ¼ the new price if the burners are still in ok shape and they are clean. Sell the propane tanks separately for $12 if empty and $20 if full.

#65-Dreck and everything else

The term "dreck" is so appropriate. It means JUNK! You WILL have lots of junk at your sale, and after the sale is over. Crummy non-descript prints and oil pictures should be priced to move for $5-10. Plastic flowers can be worth something in the right neighborhood. Old sheets and linens will have a market with the day workers. They will also try to buy half used cans of cleaning supplies. Remember this, don't sell all the toilet paper!!! A friend of mine in real estate used to say: "There is a butt for every chair" This also applies to all the dreck. Someone will take it away if the price is low enough. You want them to pay you money to help empty the house.

#66-The Art of Bargaining

We always have a sign posted at our sales: "Excessive Hagglers Will Be Asked to Leave". That doesn't mean that there can't be some wiggle room. From 15 years of experience, there are some people who are excessive hagglers. Here is one of their tricks. They will bring 20 items forward and want a discount. They will then remove 5 items and say: "Now how much". They will continue to mess with the amount of what they might buy until they wear you down. DON'T DEAL AT ALL WITH THEM! Tell them to pay the marked price or leave. They are a drain to the sale. They may become loud to intimidate you and make other buyers nervous. That is where the security doorman is again valuable. Have him escort them off the property. Make sure that there is very little price adjustment to your already low prices during the beginning of the sale. If someone wants a $10 item for $8, you can decide. If someone wants a huge discount, have them make an offer.

My rule of thumb in bargaining is that if you are being offered at least ½ of your marked price, you can start to bargain. Offers below that are a waste of time. If you reach a stumbling point, you can use lines like: "If a dollar is important to you, you know it is important to me." Or: "We have a financial responsibility to our client to bring in the most money possible." Here is another example. Your price is $10 and they offer $6. You can say: "I would feel a lot better if it were $7." Keep the buyer in the game to milk the most you can from them!

#67-Lists for Buyers

Depending on how many high priced items you are offering in your sale, always have an Offer List on all days of the sale. Even if you think the offer is ridiculous, it might be the only offer you get. Have the person put his contact information down with the price offered for your prized "white elephant". After the first day of the sale, you may want to call the person who made the offer if you will be discounting prices during the second or final days.

If you are collecting a buyers list for future sales, have a contact information list for your customers to sign up. Our list grew to be over 1000 in 15 years. These were people who liked the way we ran our sales and wanted to come back if we had another one. They will be loyal and having this list is a bargaining point when you do another interview for a new sale.

The third list is a Wish List for buyers. You may not have what they are looking for that day, but at the sale next month, you might. Let your customers tell you what they are looking for.

#68-Things to Remember- First Day of Sale

Firstly, make sure that you leave a sign-up sheet for the buyers the night before. This is how you will determine the order of who gets in first. Make sure that your workers know to show up ½ hour before the sale starts. When they show up, have them go around and look at everything that is for sale so they can direct anyone to anything, or return the item to its place if it gets carried away and dumped. If you have side gates in the yard, where someone could walk off with something undetected, lock them. The cashier needs to have a cash box with $150 in change. We found 3 twenties, 4 tens, 5 fives and 25 singles was the right mix. The garage guy will eventually need around $30 in change: a ten, 2 fives and 10 singles. After the first 2 hours, things will have slowed down to the point where he can operate independently from the house. Make sure all signs leading to the sale are up. Post all signs at the sale that show bulk prices and no excessive haggling allowed. Check to see that you have bags and boxes for your buyers. Packing material, even just newspaper, is also handy. Have the doorman/security person go out and explain to the buyers the ground rules (covered below) 5 minutes before you open the doors to anyone. Depending on the size of the house, when you open, only let in what seems comfortable, usually 10 people. The doorman will then only let in as many as have left the sale from the first group.

#69-Ground Rules

Here is typically what a doorman will say to the buyers 5 minutes before the sale opens.
"Thank you all for coming. Has everyone signed the sheet to get into the sale? Large coats and large purses need to be checked with me at the door. We will be letting in the first 10 names on the list in about 5 minutes. As people leave, we will allow more people in. As this IS the first day of the sale, our prices are FIRM! If you wish to make a lower offer for something, use the offer sheet at the cashier's desk. If you buy something large, you need to provide the movers. Our staff can't help you. (this is because having staff help a buyer move something out will remove them from their assigned duties that are more important) If you wish to be notified of our future sales, leave your contact information on the mailing list at the cashier's desk."

#70-Forms of Payment

Of course you will accept cash. If that is all you will accept, add that announcement to the "ground rules" so you don't have people waiting in line with checks and credit cards. That also should have been added to your online ad weeks before. At times our company has accepted checks when we knew the people or if it was for a very small amount and with proper ID. Otherwise, don't accept them. You can sign up to accept credit cards with a company called Square. They sent us a card-reader that fit in our cell phone. They charge 4% of the sale so you have to add that onto the total the buyer pays. You can see the charge immediately online and they will credit it to your bank account within 24 hours. For credit card sales, we charged the buyer state tax. For cash sales, we paid the tax for the buyer.

#71-The First Hour

If you can imagine the once a year Bargain Basement Sale at Macys in New York, this comes close. Even though you only let in 10 people, they will run around like head-less chickens. They will make piles of their stuff that others will take away from if they leave their pile unguarded. They will ask your staff to watch their pile. The staff has to decline. Otherwise, your staff can't keep their eyes on what the other chickens are doing. You are there for the sale, not the buyers. Even if the doorman has announced that the prices are firm, these vampires will want a discount. You can thank reality TV for that. All you need to say is: "This is the first hour of the first day of the sale. The prices are firm. If you want it for less, make an offer on the offer sheet". If several people want the same item, the offer sheet works like a silent auction. The buyers might complain about that. My wife likes the idea of a "private offer" so you won't hear the complaints. You be the judge.

The first hour is where the cashier can be overwhelmed. They have to be sure and steady and not rushed. It helps if one roamer can assist. If a buyer gets to the cashier and wants to bargain, have the cashier say NO! OR, send them to the back of the line. They may dump their pile at the cashiers and walk if they can't bargain. Your roamer can put the stuff back. When this happens, and it does happen, be aware that the buyer has removed items from the sale that others can't buy. Don't mark anything sold until there is some form of payment. Don't hold anything for a buyer who just needs to go to an ATM. We had some buyers who never came back and that item was out of the sale for the whole day. Buyers change

38

their minds. They can be selfish. Have them leave a deposit or their first born child. Something they need to come back for. Otherwise you may never see them again.

#72-After The First Hour

You have made it through the first and most challenging hour. Here are things to look for. If you were a buyer who just walked in, would the sale look neat and organized, or as if a cyclone hit the house? Have the roamers go around and straighten up everything. If pricing labels have disappeared, replace them. Make the sale looks fresh! If there isn't a line to get in outside, this is the time to let the Garage Guy go it on his own. Make it a separate venue. He will need a running tally and price tags. Remind him to say: "Hi, welcome to the sale. These are just the garage items. Everything in the house is for sale". Also remind him that he shouldn't hold anything for anyone without payment or a deposit. Ask the Cashier if he/she needs a restroom break. Gage if it will be ok to have the door open to all comers at this point. Sometimes it takes 2 hours before that can happen. Even afterward, people show up in waves which can crowd the sale. Don't worry, you WILL know the right time to let the sale be open door.

#73-End of First Sale Day

About 20 minutes before you are scheduled to close, have the person who placed the signs on the roads leading into the sale go out and take them down. Otherwise you will have a constant stream of buyers coming in and you will not be able to close on time. If you want to stay open later than the scheduled close, consider what overtime you will be paying your staff.

Again, about 20 minutes before the close, contact anyone who was going to move out furniture that they bought but still hasn't shown up. Let them know you are closing and they need to be there soon or pick up their purchase the next day. Remind them that they need to have their people to move anything heavy. My wife and I waited as much as ½ hour after the close to let some buyers pick-up a large purchase, but we didn't involve our staff. If you are running a company, that eats into your profits.

When the signs are down, announce to any buyers present that you are closing and how much time they have left to buy. Close the doors on time and pay the staff. Make sure all doors and windows are locked before you leave. They sometimes have a way of opening themselves during the sale. Remove and take with you any valuable items like sterling, or gold. Remember to leave a sign-up sheet for the next day's sale.

#74-Discounts on Later Sale Days

Most companies will discount items that haven't sold on the first day. If your sale is running 3 days, you don't really need to discount until the last day. On the second day of a 3 day sale, you can be more generous in your bargaining. If someone offers $7 for a $10 item, take it after pretending that you are giving it away at that price. You could offer BIG WHITE ELEPHANT FURNITURE at a 25% discount on the second day of a 3 day sale.

On the final day of the sale it is not uncommon for most companies to offer all merchandise at ½ price, 50% off! Of course we aren't suggesting that you sell any precious metal below its melt value. You want all of the DRECK to be gone! Again remember: THE BUYERS ARE PAYING YOU TO CLEAN OUT THE HOUSE!

#75-The Close-Out Buyer

A close out buyer is someone who will come in on the last day at the sale's close and select the "cream of the crap" that is left over. There will be lots of stuff left over from every sale and some of it will have value. Close-out buyers typically pay the estate 10 cents on the dollar of the original first day price. They provide another source of revenue for the estate. Some companies or staff of companies "become" the close out buyer to augment their bottom line. Usually the left-overs will be sold by the close-out buyer at a flea market or on all of the internet sources such as Ebay or Craigslist.

#76-End of Sale

You have finally closed the doors on your sale! Now what? If this is just an estate sale and not a pack out, you need to straighten up the house. It needs to look somewhat as it did before the sale. It needs to be broom clean. At that point, a company will extract all of their equipment from the venue and return items to shelves and clothes to the closet. That is the end of their involvement. They will go home to balance the books and produce a final settlement for the client from the agreed percentage. They will also provide the client with a copy of the running tally.

If this is a "Pack Out" which will cost extra, the company will bag all clothes and box all remaining items for donation. They will contact a charity and meet them to supervise the removal of all donations. They will arrange for a Dumpster and load the remaining junk, no one wants, into it. They will leave the house empty and broom clean. If the client needs it better than broom clean, they will contact a cleaning service and supervise that. The cost of this extra service is taken out of the client' percentage from the final tally.

.

#77-Balancing the Books

At the end of each sale day, and also the end of the sale, the company should balance the books. A good company will have the total amount from each day listed in the final summary. It should include how much cash, checks, and credit card sales happened each day. That amount needs to balance with the running tally. The final settlement needs to have the total from each day with the grand total. Before the percentage split is figured, any extra expenses like extraordinary clean up or pack out services needs to be subtracted from the client's percentage. As an example: The sales grand total was 10,000. The extra expenses ran to $900. The split is figured as $3,500 for the company. The client's split is $6,500 less the $900 cost of extra expenses, or $5,400. The client should receive a copy of the running tally as well as a total sheet with the amount they receive at the bottom. And don't forget to place the check for that amount in the envelope!!!

#78-Bank Deposit Issues

Our company used Chase Bank. They have certain limits on cash deposits within a month or you will be charged for it. This is because of all the drug cash that is floating around these days. With Chase, you can't deposit more than $7,500 in cash during one month without being charged extra. Once you go past $10,000 deposited in one month, they are required to notify the IRS. This only applies to cash. Checks and credit cards aren't counted in your deposits. If your company needs to pay less than $10,000 to the client, no problem. Just keep the left over cash in your home safe. Deposit it next month or pay for things in cash. Another way to avoid this potential problem is to find out if the client will accept cash as payment rather than a company check. Many clients prefer cash, thank God.

In conclusion, there are certain ideas to remember in this business. Some of these are obvious such as be clean, well dressed and friendly. Before, during and afterward, having patience IS a virtue. Make sure you have the right equipment and size of staff for the job. If you are a company, make sure your staff knows all of the above as well. You can create a company look if everyone has on a black shirt or top during the sale. It just looks professional. Make sure the venue is secure before, during and after the sale. Keep remembering these few things: 1-You are sellers, not repair people (tightening a screw, gluing something, or touching up a finish is ok) 2-Be kind to buyers but be on your guard as well. 3-Remember that the buyers are paying you money to clean out the house so keep your prices fair to low. 4-From small sales to large, it all adds up. 5-You are there to move the merchandise, not have a museum. If you can do all of that, you will have a great Estate Sale. I wish you many happy days of sailing!!!

www.ingramcontent.com/pod-product-compliance
Lightning Source LLC
Chambersburg PA
CBHW071144280526
45787CB00003B/1396